An American Tragedy—
"The Great Recession":

Poetic Times From Wall Street To Main Street ©

John K. Hulett

authorHOUSE®

AuthorHouse™ LLC
1663 Liberty Drive
Bloomington, IN 47403
www.authorhouse.com
Phone: 1-800-839-8640

Published by AuthorHouse 10/30/2013

ISBN: 978-1-4567-5346-7 (e)
ISBN: 978-1-4567-5347-4 (hc)
ISBN: 978-1-4567-5348-1 (sc)

Library of Congress Control Number: 2011904250

Dedication

to
Katherine and Nadia,
who endured so much during these most difficult times.
The natural man does not accept what is taught by the
Spirit of God. For him, that is absurdity. He cannot come
to know such teaching because it must be appraised in a
spiritual way. The spiritual man, on the other hand, can
appraise everything, though he himself can be appraised
by no one, for "Who has known the mind of the Lord so as
to instruct him?" But we have the mind of Christ.
1 Corinthians 2:14-16 (NAB)

to
Main Street America
and the millions of jobless and homeless Americans
devastated by the Great Recession. Your constitutional
rights for equality, justice, freedom, and the opportunity
to live with dignity shall not be denied based on race, color,
origin, age, gender, disability, or religion.

Contents

Quotes to Ponder

One of the great features of our democracy is that you and some of your friends can spend three and a half million to defeat me in an election and then, after it's over, invite me for dinner.

Governor Mark Dayton of Minnesota

This is real money that is going to make a real difference in people's lives.

President Barack Obama

*Now poverty is reaching up and
snatching people down into it.*

Robert Odom,
President of Love Incorporated,
Minneapolis, MN.

For a healthy stock market, we need bustling Main Streets and a growing, thriving middle class.

President Barack Obama

The other aspect of the unemployment rate that really concerns me is that more than 40 percent of the unemployed have been unemployed for six months or more. And that's unusually high. And people who are unemployed for such a long time, their skills erode. Their attachment to the labor force diminishes, and it may be a very, very long time before they find themselves back in a normal working position.

Federal Reserve Chairman Ben Bernanke

About the Author

John K. Hulett was living the American dream as a small business entrepreneur a few years prior to the Nation's financial crisis and hard-hitting recession. The aftermath of September 11th (2001) dramatically changed everything in the market making it impossible to full-fill orders, finance inventory, and meet financial obligations of the business. Unfortunately, Hulett was forced to close down his business due to the fact Small Business Administration (SBA) along with Wells Fargo Bank (Preferred SBA Lender) stopped supporting/financing inventory needed to keep his company operating. Unlike failed Wall Street banks the government considered *too big to fail* my business was labeled too small to succeed. Even though small business owners risk everything they have and are required to sign personal guarantees as security in case the business fails. On the other hand, CEO's from Wall Street and large public corporations are rewarded millions for failing and without ever taking risk or meeting bank/government demands for personal guarantees.

Trying to find gainful employment in a jobless economy over the past several years has been fruitless. Underemployment and unemployment were the only options available for Hulett and other middle-age struggling men and women in Minneapolis. Another option was finding new areas of interests, learning new skills and/or going back to school. Rather than sit idle and become overly critical and pessimistic about the future, Hulett opted for college. Creating more personal debt with the addition of student loans was not an ideal choice. Despite the challenges of starting over late in life and going back to school after being away for over thirty years Hulett decided to reinvest in himself securing necessary financial aid and student loans. Like most American college students, Hulett was hopeful the earned degrees would pay-off one day. Unfortunately, that has not been the case as millions of people still remain jobless and in debt including both younger and older college graduates.

John K. Hulett has more than 31 years of experience in sales, marketing, new product development, territorial expansion for manufacturing, wholesale distribution, and mass retail promotion. He has managed company branch locations and corporate divisions at the regional and national level. Hulett has also spent time as a small business entrepreneur establishing start-up companies, developing numerous business and marketing plans, securing multiple patents, trademarks, trade names, and copy rights. He has a Master of Arts in Theological Studies, Bachelor of Science in Business Management, Certificate in Human Resource Management, Certificate in Small Business Management, Certificate in Marketing Management, Certificate in International Business, and Associate of Science Degree in

Individualized Studies. An American Tragedy—"The Great Recession": Poetic Times from Wall Street to Main Street is his second book. His first book AGE DISCRIMINATION: AN EPIDEMIC IN AMERICA AFFECTING PEOPLE OF ALL AGES highlights Age Discrimination and its Effects in the Workplace.

The Author

John Hulett was inspired by personal and family tragedy brought on by the worst economic crisis in a generation. For many, the devastating effects of this recession linger bitterly year after year, with no end in sight. Several years of underemployment and unemployment have created impoverished conditions for millions of Americans, while government standards still rely on statistics from the 1960s. Opportunities for securing gainful employment in Minnesota—that is, full-time jobs offering benefits and livable wages—have been slim for far too long. Hopes for a recovering economy remain optimistic only based on one's ambition, motivation, and creative drive for independence. For many middle-age men and women, this is the only means of survival available.

An American Tragedy—*"The Great Recession"* is about living through alienation, rejection, and loss of everything, including family and friends. Drowning in a failed economy paralyzes the will to live, but finding poetic justice and compassion in the human heart is a small form of healing. The sufferings of millions of families living in poverty in this nation, many without work or a place to live, are not only criminal, they are inhumane and unacceptable in present-day

America. The United States needs every available citizen who is physically able and willing to work if it is going to emerge from its multi-trillion-dollar debt crisis.

His first book, *Age Discrimination: An Epidemic in America Affecting People of All Ages* (AuthorHouse, 2010, 2011), chronicles five failed investigations prompted by Hulett's lawsuit claiming age discrimination. Hulett details how the government participated in these investigations and how large corporations are protected from employee claims because of their close relationships with many government agencies. He also thoroughly examined the correlation between today's deep recession and age discrimination.

A few years prior to the Great Recession, Hulett was operating a small distribution business. His combined experience of more than thirty years in new business (startup) formation, new product design and development, sales, marketing, and management of both regional and national territories for manufacturers, wholesale distribution, dealer/contractor rental stores, and mass-retail chains enabled him to live the American dream. In addition, Hulett orchestrated numerous business and marketing plan proposals, developed proprietary technology, and secured copyrights, patents, trademarks, and trade names for private companies.

At age 50 Hulett went back to school after being away for over thirty years. He completed a Master of Arts in Theological Studies with emphasis on Apologetics; a Bachelor of Science in Business Management; Certificates in Human Resource

Management, Small Business Management, Marketing Management, International Business; and an Associate of Science Degree in Individualized Studies with emphasis on Entrepreneurial Leadership.

Perhaps the most meaningful of Hulett's achievements has been reaching a spiritual milestone of twenty-five silent/reflective retreats with men of faith in July of 2010. To omit faith as a vital component in helping overcome adversities such as those chronicled in this book would be an even greater tragedy. In fact, it would be impossible for most, given the circumstances.

Introduction

America's economy continues to idle in recession mode while millions of unemployed breathe a sigh of relief as Congress finally passed a vote (59—39) approving another extension of jobless benefits. Political roadblocks from the partisan minority led to months of delays. President Obama stated, "Americans who are working day and night to get back on their feet and support their families in these tough economic times deserve more than obstruction and partisan game-playing." Once again, well-spoken words provide a glimmer of hope for those in need of some form of delayed compassion. Perhaps what is truly missing in all this economic chaos and partisan politics are bits and pieces of poetic justice. After all, once the $34 billion six-month extension has been fully funded to aid the 2.5 million people who have been out of work for six months or more, Congress will have to figure out what to do with the other forgotten group: the millions left behind who are still unemployed with no benefits and the unknown numbers of underemployed who have not been able to cover basic living expenses since early 2007.

Having felt and still feeling the wrath of this Great Recession myself, I find it difficult to argue against some type of government aid for those of us in need. Most unemployed and underemployed people in America are not expecting a welfare handout from the government (taxpayers). A job that pays a livable wage and reasonable benefits is all we seek. Is that too much to expect by the citizens of a country so rich and prosperous as the United States? How will it be possible to create jobs and strengthen the economy if some of our leaders in Washington oppose incentives to do so? If the facts, data, and outrage from Wall Street's behavior have not gotten through to our leaders, then maybe it is time to send a message from Main Street to Washington by way of poetry. This book is dedicated to the millions of Americans who have lost their jobs, homes, life savings, benefits, families, and friends since the Great Recession began. I live your pain every day. Please do not forget that your struggles and sufferings are also mine. We walk this road together in hopes of building a stronger America today and tomorrow.

Vision comes alive
when everyone sees where his or her
contribution makes a difference.
Ken Blanchard, John P. Carlos, and Alan Randolph

American Tragedy #1

Once upon a time, a prosperous nation fell into a Great Recession, and its people cried out, "We are hurting. Can somebody please help us?"

No hard feelings folks, it's just business as usual: Rich and powerful leaders running the financial affairs of Wall Street and politicians campaigning for re-election are too focused on their own "me" agendas.

"But wait a minute. Don't you know millions of Americans are standing in food lines hoping to receive a bag or two of rationed goods?"

Private jets taxi down airport runways waiting for clearance from control towers as the elite talk among themselves. Exotic investments, iconic museums, and lavish vacations for them; for the poor and oppressed, jobs, homes, and dreams that have all but vanished like smoke.

The lines are getting longer each day as daylight hours grow shorter and temperatures fall for the poor and hungry. A man with no teeth smiles and says, "I'm eighty years, and I'm old standing in line for food to feed my family; is this the Great Depression all over again?"

A voice from farther down the line shouts, "No, this is the Great Recession of 2010—get a grip, old man!"

Idle chatter continues as concerns among the poor stir chants: "No jobs! No food! No place to live!" Jesus spoke of the poor as always being around and in need of compassion. Can this be happening today, here in America? I thought President Johnson declared a war on poverty back in 1964.

Voices whispering through the pines spill harsh words of poison: "Children born into poverty breed a life of poverty." I can still hear children singing, "Poverty and me are pretty good company." I hope someone finds them soon, for they truly are the forgotten ones, hidden in large cities and small towns across America. Yes, they are the poor and faceless beggars who cry out like hungry wolves in the night. How tragic is the Great Recession that there are families from all walks of life living on the edge? No one seems to notice their shabby clothes and dirty shoes. "Feed America," "Feed My Starving Children," "Food for the Poor," and "Ignore the Hungry/Homeless No More" are common themes for today's outreach in America. Some people wish they would all just go away.

Where have all the institutions gone? Over forty million Americans living in poverty while one out of every five children is labeled poor. It is truly an American Tragedy, an American Tragedy, an American Tragedy . . . .

American Tragedy #2:
Bail out the Boys

They say it was done to protect the American people. We were warned: "Beware: Fragile Economy. Extraordinary measures must be taken."

Henry, we couldn't have done it without you.
Thanks for the billions—
Lots of love from Wall Street.

Bail out the boys, America, for they are in need of our help.

"Madam Speaker, a breakfast meeting tomorrow will not do. We must meet for wine and cheese now!" What are the symptoms of this economic disaster? Just a mild heart attack and a few clogged arteries, that's all. Thanks for the "fragile" update, Henry. See you soon. Congress gave the nod and Henry the Negotiator was off and running to save America. A mere $700 billion. (Or was it $800 billion?) It was at least enough to give Wall Street some breathing room for the day. Bail out the boys, America, for they are in need of our help.

Where were the SEC regulators when the people needed them most? Did they not see the warning signs years ago? American taxpayers were forced to swallow millions of dollars in toxic loans, thanks to failed Wall Street. No one wanted these exotic mortgages, so we swallowed them up for Henry. Bail out the boys, America, for they are in need of our help.

Turbulence and turmoil pummeled our failed financial system as we watched A.I.G, Goldman Sachs, Lehman Brothers, and WAMU tumble down. In the meantime, A.I.G. made their lavish $400,000 getaway while Merrill Lynch conducted a priceless office makeover for its CEO. Not to be outdone, Wall Street paid out $18 billion in year-end CEO bonuses. Bail out the boys, America, for they are in need of our help.

American Tragedy #3: CEO Watch Alert

The American people feel the pain at the pump as they check their pockets for spare change, gift vouchers, and discount coupons. But where are the jars filled with nickels and dimes? Pump #7 please accept my apologies for the $5.00's in change. Do CEOs ever worry about paying for gas? I imagine the recession must be stressful on them. How do they look, act, and feel inside when mingling with the middle/low class people who are just struggling to hang on?

For some, the recession must be quite humbling: a painful cut in pay, smaller bonuses, and fewer stock options to count. Not to worry: no doubt, the board will come through with a package to cover those losses. If push comes to shove, would you settle for a little less than $7.6 million? Not to worry: the board will make up the difference with more perks and bigger incentives next year. It saddens me so to see grown men cry. Cascading waterfalls running down the faces of three hundred fearless CEOs is heartbreaking.

Cheer up, all you CEOs who earned less than $10 million last year: more perks and increased packages will be approved soon. May the top ten achievers inspire hope for all those who fell below their customary earnings:

1. Aubrey McClendon, Chesapeake Energy—$112.5 million
2. Sanjay Jha, Motorola—$104.4 million
3. Robert Iger, Walt Disney—$51.1 million
4. Lloyd Blankfein, Goldman Sachs—$42.9 million
5. Kenneth Chenault, American Express—$42.9 million
6. Vikram Pandit, Citigroup—$38.2 million
7. Steven Farris, Apache Corp.—$37.2 million
8. Louis Camilleri, Phillip Morris—$36.9 million
9. Kevin Johnson, Juniper Networks—$36.1 million
10. Jamie Dimon, JP Morgan Chase—$35.7 million

This truly is an inspiration to those who worked so hard to stay on top of their game despite the recession and economic meltdown. Stay strong, all you CEOs, for you are America's most trusted, and don't forget to keep close watch on those liberals who are attempting to rein in your pay.

American Tragedy #4: Dying to Live

Caught in the crossfire of race, poverty, and no county program for heat-share this year—just my father, a friend, and me. Emergency funds from the government ran dry, there was no money to spare and no one to care. Oh, how I wish Christmas were here with a warm shelter and a furnace filled with heat to melt the ice off our chair.

Our meal today was a loaf of moldy bread and potted meat from a can. The smell reminds me of the dog food we ate yesterday. What does it take to get a break in this life? So fragile are we. There are days when I miss my mother, my father, a friend, and me.

The chill from broken glass windows was unusually cold today, but my father, I'm told, borrowed a gas generator from the neighbors. Our last supper was made of day-old breadsticks, but no one complained. If only someone had warned us about the deadly fuel and foul air mix. Such a shame: carbon monoxide poisoned our rooms. We never thought we'd die like this, not from these odorless toxic fumes.

There were no laws or rules in place to save us, no government funding available to aid us. After all, there was too much to do on Wall Street and nothing leftover to help the poor on Main Street. If only we had lived for just one more day, perhaps the government could have found another way. Dying to live is not so bad, you see, for God was waiting patiently for my father, a friend, and me.

American Tragedy #5: Shedding Jobs Forever

They say the worst of the economy crash and job market collapse is over, but the country keeps shedding more jobs daily. Over 8 million jobs disappeared since the recession devoured the nation. They say millions more could follow. How will the unemployed ever find jobs in America again? Perhaps trillions of dollars in deficit financing, massive tax cuts, stimulus packages, and more . . . .

No one really knows what the true unemployment rate is. It could be 9.8 percent, 16.4 percent, 24.4 percent, or more. They say 26.2 million Americans are underemployed, while others have just given up looking for work. Percentages don't really matter; they say the economy shed another 345,000 in May. The Labor Department worries America's 14.5 million unemployed face a tough go ahead. No jobs for the restless and worried so sad.

Companies are not hiring as they brace for the worst, yet the longer they delay hiring America's unemployed, profits will rise while management adapts to less personnel. Job losses are down considerably from the 504,000 in April. Hilda's still not happy with the unemployment news. She feels the unemployed need new skills and retraining. Ben, on the other hand, is confident the recession will be over by year's end.

Census Bureau pumped a little false hope into the economy for 2010. They say 1.2 million (part-time) temporary workers were hired for the season, and $11 billion in cash was spent. At least it was something for a small percentage of the unemployed standing in food lines. The good news is, when all's said and done, the poor and disabled may get some funds, and laborers will have short-term jobs building a few more schools and prisons. It's so sad. You see, on this Labor Day weekend, 15 million unemployed sit idle, wishing they had something to do. Too little too late.

American Tragedy #6: TARP Fishing

Dear Mr. Treasury,

We understand the federal watchdog is overseeing the pond resources as more than six hundred banks come nibbling for chunks and pieces of taxpayer bailout dollars. Where did the $800 billion go? After a series of inquiries and surveys were made, a flurry of responses finally trickled down. Not many loans, if any, were made to boost our failed economy. You must have some idea where at least $330 billion in TARP (Troubled Asset Relief Program) funds went. No?

American International Group (A.I.G.) is doing just fine, we hear, as they maneuver through unsupervised waters with $180 billion in TARP funding. We, the people of America, have a right to know where the money went, do we not? Show us at least where 80 percent has gone. You owe the taxpayers that much. Oh, and thanks for the fishing memories; the poor and the homeless truly cherish them all:

- Goldman Sachs—$12.9 billion
- Merrill Lynch—$6.8 billion
- Bank of America—$5.2 billion

- Citigroup—$2.3 billion
- Wachovia—$1.5 billion

Please note: the American people are so relieved to know TARP is feeding the banks of Europe as well:

- Societe of Generale of France—$12 billion
- Deutsche Bank of Germany—$12 billion
- Barclays of Britain—$8.5 billion
- USB of Switzerland—$5 billion

Last, some of us were concerned A.I.G.'s $165 million in bonuses had not yet been paid out for a job well done. Please advise at your earliest convenience.

Respectfully,
Jobless American Taxpayers

P.S.   How is Wells Fargo doing with its $25 billion in TARP funding? We noticed Wells Fargo acquired Wachovia, who also received $1.5 billion in TARP funds. We hope this will help motivate them to lend to small businesses soon.

American Tragedy #7: Greed for the Greater Good

A decade of historical greed, corruption, and fraud has done little or no good for the American people. However, how would the average person ever know he or she could achieve such great wealth and success without our leaders failing so miserably? The recent economic disaster proves that one can still receive perks and rewards shamelessly through defiance and government immunity.

Yes, America, Wall Street showed us that dreams and nightmares can come true, yet still have happy endings. Lavish vacations occurred for many while luxury jets filled runways and production schedules. Greed truly showed us what's possible if only we open our eyes to see. It's all relative: what is good for you is toxic for me.

Executives received millions in bonuses and compensation packages while denying and claiming ignorance of failures in their companies. The President even forced some to resign and still left with a bagful of millions. No one did jail time for their failures and gross mismanagement of financial investments. They failed for the greater good.

If one takes but a moment to reflect on all the greed that has taken place in this country, there is still hope for the poor, hungry, homeless, and wrongfully imprisoned. It appears the greater good always comes from the most dishonest and deceptive of people.

American Tragedy #8:
Jobless in America

Lost my self-esteem along the way—can't even find family or friends to help push a broken down car off the road. This jobless nightmare has to end soon. I've been saying this for far too many years. Begging and borrowing from everyone—it's no wonder my wife drove away in tears. Caught a double dose of depression the other day. What worries me most: anxiety migraines never go away.

Family in crisis, forced to sell their home, harassed by numerous collection agencies, never left alone. Home value and equity diminishes by the day. Pressures from the market—my, how my agent loves to play. It's been two years, and no offers have been made. Bitterness lingers; few words, rarely spoken.

Hundreds of resumes have gone out since the recession began. Still no response from employer ads though thousands ran. It's difficult to know if a job even exists, but I keep applying, though I'd rather resist. Some say job-seekers need to reinvent themselves: dye your hair, lose weight, and get a wardrobe makeover. When I think about all that was lost and shelved, I'd rather commit myself—let an institution take over the hopeless.

Politicians are flooding the media with trash talk and trendy job slogans while knocking on neighborhood doors touting creative economic proposals. Too many false hopes for green futures unknown. Oh, why do these folks only come around re-election time? Candidates running for office, you see, have trouble distinguishing between gainfully employed and jobless people like me.

American Tragedy #9:
Ponzi Me

Too shrewd and too slick to be uncovered for years, while most are caught for traffic violations and charged immediately. Where were the watchdogs when the mastermind swindled $65 billion? Red flags waving in the wind for over sixteen years, yet SEC regulators could see no fraud. Do we lack competence or is there favoritism here in the system?

Thanks, Harry, you're a genius. You figured out Bernie's scheme in five minutes or less while SEC appeared baffled for years. Your whistle-blowing over the past five years did not go unnoticed. The people who lost everything applaud your investigative efforts and ability to help the government admit its failures in the case.

Only in America can one pull off such a Ponzi of this magnitude and still cut a deal with SEC that allows you not to admit or deny allegations for a civil complaint. Bernie certainly will go down in history as one of the greatest scam artists of all time. A 150-year sentence for a Ponzi scheme that devoured the life savings of thousands seems like a long time for a man in his sixties. At least Bernie will have ample time to ponder his financial affairs.

American Tragedy #10:
Too Big to Fail

In the economy today, they say size really matters. Bernie never would have pulled off such a grand scheme if this were not true. The government stood shocked, overwhelmed, and imperiled 'til someone decided these American icons were too big to fail. They doubled the nets for the big ones to leap, then down came Fannie, Freddie, and Bear, along with GM, AIG, Wachovia, and Chrysler in a Jeep.

We don't know if anyone ever took blame for the financial chaos they caused this great nation, but we knew when world billionaires Buffet, Helu', and Gates shifted rank and location. Amazing the three richest men in the world, have combined such wealth—$180 billion strong. Once they finally top a trillion, would controlling the world's greatest wealth be so wrong?

Perhaps some will always wonder, "What if we allowed them to fail?" Do we assume no one else is competent, or are we just a bit too frail? What Wells Fargo, Citibank, and Bank America lack—Ford, Merrill Lynch, and Toyota will bring back. Eight hundred billion was a lot, you see, for bailing out the brilliant men who bankrupt you and me.

American Tragedy #11: Too Small to Succeed

Living the American dream not so long ago was a promise of hope for those hungry for independence. The small businessman was the one with the least, yet willing to risk it all to create opportunity in America. Loans and personal guarantees were a part of the plan, and no one ever questioned, not even the small businessman.

There was a hidden code to operate ethically and return what was borrowed—live morally. A day came when the bank called in the note, unwilling to renegotiate prior terms they wrote. Many calls and meetings were held to find alternative sourcing. The building owner sued and locked the doors—a major victory. Attorneys served papers and secured documents as a means for credibility. Loans and personal guarantees were a part of the plan no one ever questioned, not even the small businessman.

Everything ended in up bankruptcy as the courts seized bank accounts, and assets were all stripped clean. No investors, bankers, or government officials were ever seen. Nothing was left behind except bits and pieces of a broken American dream. It may seem unfair compared to Wall

Street, but that's just the way it is for the small businessman living on Main Street. Loans and personal guarantees were a part of the plan no one ever questioned, not even the small businessman.

American Tragedy #12:
Fraud Countless

News that made fraud history in this country over the past decade has given me a headache. Enron, Arthur Anderson, World Comm, and so much more; the list of names is endless, yet many executives who commit these crimes every day fair exceptionally well. Why bother counting the mundane? So much that was fraud yesterday has become cultural norm today.

What about those who defraud American taxpayers out of $60 billion annually in Medicare and Medicaid billing scams? No problem: let the media cover it for a story or two, and perhaps the government will become a reactive enforcer. Too much to count—too little to cover with fraud resources, they say.

It's not often lawyers hit the fraud news wire; hats off to Manhattan attorney Marc Dreier for admitting he played a seven-year $400 million scheme. The talk of a 145-year prison term was a bit much for a man of this profession, so they settled for 20 just the same. Engulfed in a master Ponzi with no way out pales in comparison to the victims stripped of their lives' savings and left homeless to die.

No one is immune from the shame and fallout of this tragic disease. Business Mogul Tom Petters built an empire of $3.65 billion in fraud with a little Minnesota pride on the side. Local politicians scurried to wash their hands of Petters' $400,000 political donations. Does thirty years to life really matter when sentenced at age 52?

American Tragedy #13: Tears of My Father

He hasn't been himself lately—quiet and withdrawn. Could it be a touch of flu or possibly anxiety from not much to do? A neighbor stopped by the house the other day to see if he was around. Never answered the door—not even the dog made a sound. Each day passes, and still no news on the streets. Where are all the jobs they promised so long ago?

Misled by politicians canvassing neighborhoods begging for votes; the phone seldom rings accept for collectors and hang-up calls. Remember the happy times, lively conversations in the halls? The house feels so empty now with no one around. A few outside lights, burned-out it seems careless to me. Wish this God-forsaken house would sell and set him free.

Caught someone peeping through my window this past Sunday morning. What was he hoping to find? Trash talk here and ridicule there—idle ignorance is so unkind. The dog is aging, crippling sadly; she loses control, dreaming of sights, sounds, and smells of the trails we once walked on so long ago. It's three in the morning. Someone's crying downstairs; must be the dog or the night wind. Who really cares?

American Tragedy #14: Living the Dream Homeless

A woman and her two children stopped by the old church the other day. They were looking for food and shoes, and had something to say. Lost her job, evicted from an apartment, family in despair. Open the doors of compassion, and offer your place to share. One bedroom is all that they had; if only she could find shelter from the storm, she'd be glad. Homeless schoolchildren left holding empty bags while government assistance continually drags. Politicians too busy salvaging careers; poverty, oppression, and rising shelter fears. A candlelight vigil held one night late, remembering the 134 who died without hate.

American Tragedy #15: Admit No Wrong

Why are some people granted such immunity, never willing to admit their wrong? Average citizens found guilty are charged for their crimes immediately. Lawyers defend corporations and government entities to no avail. Fraud, racism, and human rights charges headline the news. Why do they pay out multi-million dollar settlements with stipulations that let them deny any wrongdoing? Just ponder the mix of the following news:

- Gateway Funding Diversified Mortgage Services, Equal Credit Opportunity violations—fined $2.7 million and admitted no wrongdoing
- City of Minneapolis Police, twenty-year history of racism—settled for $740,000 and acknowledged no discrimination
- United Health CEO William McGuire, fraud—settled for $30 million to the class action, $7 million to the SEC, and $618 in relinquished benefits without admitting wrongdoing

- Bernie Madoff—cut a deal with the SEC in a civil complaint without admitting or denying allegations

Some criminals will always have options to choose—win or lose.

American Tragedy #16: Foreclosure Today, For Sale Tomorrow

Remember the days when the great bubble appeared to have no end in sight? Investments piled billions upon billions. Sub-prime mortgages—exotic ones—packaged and sold by the brightest on Wall Street. Alt-As and optional ARMs lured them in by the thousands to bigger homes and lower payments with no qualifications. Wouldn't one think the least credit-worthy borrowers would trend to mass default sooner or later? Now look what we have: trillions of dollars in mortgage failures, all because of obsession and deception. Poor families are forced out in great numbers as foreclosure companies clean up. From Florida to California and all states in between, no one is immune from this great foreclosure tragedy. Where will they ever find qualified buyers in the near future? Not here or there, not in this free-falling market.

American Tragedy #17: Stimulus Plan

American Recovery and Reinvestment Act of 2009, we hope, helped some of those in dire need. A proposed $787 billion in new spending and tax cuts should have had some effect on the economy. Legislators said stimulus help would create jobs, assist unemployment and the uninsured, provide state budget relief, and invest in infrastructure, education, science, health, and energy efficiency. At least the first wave of unemployed enjoyed a much needed 33-week benefit extension through the end of 2009.The poorest of the poor also welcomed the increase in food stamps as well. Disadvantaged student programs and increased Pell Grants for low-income students and parents were extremely helpful for people living on the edge. A few highway projects appeared on the screen, but not much was approved in for rehabilitation of vacant and foreclosed housing. We heard little about Temporary Assistance for Needy Families or about whether the $636 million lending and loan guarantees were ever made from banks via SBA to small businesses. Supposedly, several provisions were made relating to executive compensation. The Treasury Secretary was assigned to monitor recipients of TARP funds, limit their compensation and bonuses, recover prior bonuses, and prevent golden parachutes and executive bonuses from being paid. Middle-class Americans, on the other hand, face more job and wage cuts and loss of health coverage and economic opportunity as they fight their way from the bottom to cover basic living expenses.

American Tragedy #18:
Tiers of Fears

Final extension was passed into law today; long overdue unemployment benefits for the two million who need pay. Headlines stated, "Worst Economic Conditions since the Great Depression." Still, Congressional delays force a late night confession. They had to endure more fiscal hardships, these tiers. Why do some always stir senseless political fears? Perhaps the greatest fear lawmakers avoided this session, addressing the millions still stuck in the recession. For all the unemployed who already exhausted their benefits there is nothing more the government can do. Check with social services, local outreach, and food banks; the burden is all on you. Extensions for tax breaks on the wealthiest they debate, while Tier 5 activists sit on the sidelines and wait. The House is reluctant to argue further for those out on a limb. Sorry, longest-suffering tiers, your future tragically looks grim.

American Tragedy #19: Bankrupt Me, America

Chapter 7 or 11: pick and choose your fate. You tried and tried, still failed. All is gone too late. Thousands of dollars in debt while others in millions; America's digging deeper daily by the trillions. Homeless men and women begging at the crossroads, waving signs of compassion: "God Bless, Jesus loves you." Help them. What more can they do? A fight breaks out. Turf wars begin. Stealing another man's livelihood truly is a sin. Homeless, jobless, and broke, where shall they go? Wall Street, you devil, swindled America's soul. They say forty million Americans are living in poverty while fourteen million children go hungry every day. What if all the wealth were divided up equally? Then we would not have to worry about economic disparity.

American Tragedy #20:
Fringe Benefits, Anyone?

Jobs paying poverty wages on the rise by the millions year after year, fringe benefits for the rich also rise as boardrooms' cheer after cheer. Working-class families continue to fall below the economic recovery line, while benefits and perks mount up for those doing fine. Minimum wage ranges $5.25 to $8.11, how many hours would it take to break even working 24/7? You see, the benefits some make don't really matter much to me except when millions out of work struggle to live simply.

American Tragedy #21: Poor Helping the Poor

My daughter works three part-time jobs. She's failing to get by. I, on the other hand, am unemployed, yet still willing to try. She needs help with gas, groceries, car repairs, and insurance. I give when I can. We meet every so often, poor helping the poor. Oh, why doesn't he even try to do a little bit more?

Was in a bind the other day—needed five dollars for gas. No one could help, so I dug through the trash. Bumped into a friend while on my way; found he's living paycheck to paycheck, working three hours each day. He offered me twenty, said, "Pay when you can." It makes you feel human when the poor lend a hand.

American Tragedy #22: Who's to Blame?

A decade filled with so much fraud, greed, and corruption: fingers point to one administration or the other, yet no one admits blame. Crimes of passion and adultery run deceptively out of control. Record numbers of marriages end in divorce. Nightly news softens traditional meaning. Where has our faith gone?

Agnostics and pagans attempt to sway votes in the nation as church separates farther from state. Slogans embraced everywhere: *"Diversity is good, you see; what is true for you is not for me."* Corporate ethics violations make history in America while a failed economy leaves the country in ruin. Environmental disasters plague the nation for generations. Millions live in poverty as wealth increases in the hands of select few. God is not to blame for mismanaged resources.

American Tragedy #23: Unemployed, Underemployed

Employers have reduced their labor forces since the recession began. Sales and profits are down, so go employee hours, benefits, and drastic cuts in pay. Economic warriors 12.5 million strong; they're the unemployed and underemployed who need our help moving along.

Since the recession began December 2007, 5.1 million jobs vanished, never to be replaced. No fear as they wait for Government's $787 billion stimulus to create 3.5 million new jobs. Economic warriors 15.1 million strong: they're the unemployed and underemployed who need our help moving along.

Some settled for part-time jobs; others quit looking for work that was not there. Perhaps if they knew the real unemployment rate—17.5 percent and more—it may shock the nation. Economic warriors 15.7 million strong; they're the unemployed and underemployed who need our help moving along.

Still, Wall Street investors try to focus on good news; all this talk of *Great Recession* is somewhat depressing. Jobless rates climb to 22.5 percent in Michigan—auto-industry-specific. Economic warriors over 16 million strong; they're the unemployed and underemployed who need our help moving along.

American Tragedy #24: Change Is Coming, America

What's happened in neighborhoods throughout this great country? Rows of vacant houses and foreclosure signs line the streets. Middle-class people humble themselves standing in food lines for hours. Hand-me-down clothes, garage sales, and second-hand stores have become the norm. Dollar-menu wars with fast-food chains echo deals of great value as thrifty stores on the rise make nightly news.

Too many jobless people begging on the roadsides while luxury cars and SUVs text along freeways. Unemployment at an all-time record, twenty-five-year high, still the unknown underemployment factor stirs fear. Tea parties and GOP gatherings rally for 2012 support in affluent areas. What does this all mean?

Environmental backlash, too much profiteering in the Gulf, disappointment with progress in Middle-East wars, resentments stir emotions for the apposed in building a mosque near Ground Zero. Jobless meets homeless. What is this strange charade? Poverty is on the rise by the millions as the wealthy increase net worth in billions. Economy staggers under trillions in debt, and millions still without healthcare and unemployment benefits. Banks and CEOs still prosper, despite slow recovery status. Change is coming, America, just you wait and see.

American Tragedy #25: Empty Pockets, Vacant Houses

Poverty in America hit an eleven-year high as the worst recession since the Great Depression drove millions to despair. Things were not great in 2008 as the Census Bureau posted 39.8 million Americans living in poverty. The nation's number of vacant homes increased to nineteen million; does anyone really care?

Too many people living in poverty as numbers rise another four million. Things were not fine in 2009 as the Census Bureau posted 43.6 million Americans living in poverty. The nation has 8.8 million families struggling in poverty. Does anyone need county assistance in heat-share, food, shelter, and medical coverage, too?

American Tragedy #26:
Market Soars

Dow roars back ten thousand points in the middle of a recession as Wall Street cheers on the rise in earnings for J.P. Morgan Chase. Thanks, blue chips, for showing the old surge of prior years. The U.S. economy rose a slight 0.5 percent in retail sales after a great boost in the auto industry from the stimulus funding "cash for clunkers."

Ecolab Inc. CEO Douglas Baker Jr. was all smiles. Total compensation package increased to $5,282,979, up 107 percent over prior year's $2.6 million. Citibank reports $101 million in profit as Goldman Sachs earnings triple to $3.03 billion. The bailout's working, America. Market soars on South Jersey shores.

American Tragedy #27: Where's My Taxpayer Advocate?

Waited in line over three hours. Needed to meet with a volunteer tax preparer. Single parent of two with simple deductions—nothing too complex to handle. Another two hours went by, and the file, almost complete, was informed of missing tax receipt. They advised to file electronically as is and come back another day to amend. Was in desperate need for the money. What more could one say?

Unemployed for several months, out of benefits and extensions, my family was in dire need of a small refund to live. All the files were processed per I.R.S. requirements; nothing needed to be done. Under duress, made a call to the Taxpayer Advocate Service, "Your Voice at the I.R.S." In hardship, please help! Numerous calls and messages were left, along with duplicate files and faxes. Where was our advocate when my family was in need of her help the most? Was in desperate need of the money. What more could one say?

Proof of economic hardship was well documented—all files were presented—yet Wall Street CEOs in Congressional hearings provided nothing. Four months went by, still no word on a refund. Was in desperate need of the money.

What more could one say? The first $800 billion taxpayer bailouts took less than two weeks for approval, while our $800 family hardship was delayed months. What about the guarantee I'd receive fair and unbiased review? Even my advocate assured expedited process of amended return and refund. In the end, there are no guarantees or worries on the minds of government representatives, for they will never see the faces of families suffering economic hardships. Was in desperate need of the money. What more could one say?

American Tragedy #28: A Nation in Crisis

America came close to a free-fall depression thanks to Federal Reserve Ben. We dodged that fatal bullet. Is there really such a thing as a perfect storm? Some may argue, thousands of years ago a perfect world was created.

Economy is still sluggish and slow as jobs remain scarce and obscure. Federal Trade Commission chases down Intel Corporation antitrust violations and net $1.45 billion in fines. Not so long ago Microsoft was caught jogging in similar shoes.

Justice Department settles $536 million charge with Credit Sussie Group for illegal business transactions with Iranian Banks. AIG, GMAC, Freddie Mac, and Fannie Mae cannot pay back TARP billions lent. Stress tests show they will need billions more to go. What has happened to our financial security now that we've become a nation in crisis— China's holding notes?

American Tragedy #29: A Life in Shambles

Sparse paychecks this week—I'm in between. Wish there were extra cash so things weren't so lean. My car's coasting on fumes, cell phone's shut off; think I'll stay home and clean my room. Many resumes have gone out—no replies; my father's still unemployed—feel I could die.

My mother worries I'm wasting my time holding out for jobs that fit more of my prime. Intern by day, nanny by night. Lack of resources makes me very uptight. Sure miss the days of family and home-cooked meals. How I hate staring out my bedroom window, feeling broke and alone.

American Tragedy #30: Fleecing of America

Job bias claims hit record highs as government struggles to replace millions of jobs lost in the recession. If only someone could come up with a plan to hide the graying of America. Corporations have found ways to run more efficiently using higher productivity measures and younger personnel. They have mastered discrimination laws and are free to beat the system; gatekeepers are told when to broom out the old.

Cutting wages and benefits are only part of today's norm. Reduction in hours and rising performance terminations have become employers' perfect storm. Nickel-and-diming middle-age men and women is now America's competitive edge. Where will employers go once they realize skilled labor is missing? Perhaps in the food lines or homeless shelters; wash the scared feet and beg for the skilled missing.

Forget about the 93,277 job bias claims filed with EEOC and $376 million in settlement awards. Once you eliminate age and experience, try growing the economy. Who is left to develop new commerce ideas and green technology jobs: Politicians?

American Tragedy #31: America's Back

America boasts of its achievements around the world—recovering so quickly from financial ruin. Stock markets rallied up thousands of points as the auto industry hit mid-double-digits earlier this year. Why, even the economy added 162,000 new jobs and the U.S. dollar rose, too. America's resilience is its competitive edge. No other country can absorb massive debt and erase it completely like the United States. Yes, we are the market-driven innovators. Quick turnaround and lightning abilities help us process disasters like nobody's business. Who knew profits would be up substantially—exports rising in the billions? Employment has fallen dramatically as companies become more efficient—doing more with less. Some say America's back from the recession, but it may never figure out how to replace 8.2 million jobs lost since 2007.

American Tragedy #32: Feed the Hungry

No longer do we need to look beyond our back yard, America, for the poor and hungry live here. They fill our streets, shelters, and fixed-up homes in just about every city. Where do they come from, you say—illegal immigrants? Many born and raised here in America. Recession, depression: what's the difference when over 44 million live impoverished in the nation? Congress remains divided over a bill addressing the poor in need of new standards. Make no mistake, America, food lines for the homeless are on the rise. For some, revising reports measuring poverty is too much compromise.

American Tragedy #33:
Too Little, Too Late

No one will ever know how many died along the roadside during the Great Recession. Hidden matters such as these are truly American tragedies. In fact, most will have forgotten years from now how time stood still for millions cast aside. A civil award of some kind will never due, and neither will token grants or loans for a select few. Yes, the casualties from poverty are high: scattered families and broken homes everywhere, retirements, savings, and homes completely erased. So much was lost on that dark day as outreach gave out tickets of compassion to the poor. Job benefit extensions provided relief for a few while debate over healthcare gave hope for the ill. Once an individual has been stripped of his or her humanity, all that's left is his or her faith. Had the sense of urgency equaled that of Wall Street, who knows how many families could have been saved? For the people on Main Street, it's just too little too late.

American Tragedy #34:
Disaster Zone:
BP's Oil Spill, America's Crisis

Since the invasion of crude oil in the Gulf, dark oceanic patches have become infamous to millions. Months of surging oil gushing from the ocean depths left tainted beaches all over the Gulf. Fish and birds lie dead on the shores, some coated with heavy oil, others gasping for clean air. Whose ass did BP's disaster really kick?

Fishing industry tanked as the tide opened doors to oversea imports. Can anyone blame the people for not wanting to eat seafood feared toxic and oil-tainted? Not even the FDA can instill confidence or convince people chemical dispersants pose no health threat.

The nation's worst oil spill, dumping more than 53 million gallons, is hard to accept. Listen to the logic: only a quarter of spilled oil is left on the shorelines, and the rest has either dissipated or disappeared. We don't really know. Dead fish on the shores, environmental future unknown. Will BP or America eventually clean up this mess?

American Tragedy #35:
Inside Looking Out

Dust and cobwebs obscure my view as I peer out a corner window from down below. The sound of a pin dropped in the hallway yesterday nearly pierced my ears. Birds pecking on outside walls while bats scratch from inside the closet—too much harassing noise. Whose eyes are those staring at me in the dark? Don't they know it's an invasion of my privacy?

Crashing thunder and pounding rain kept me awake last night as the wind blew red oak branches and willow leaves from the trees. Whispering voices outside my front door told me everyone's vacated the neighborhood. No one had the courtesy to notify me a silent pandemic was here. Heard banging on the windows early this morning, but when I looked out no one was there.

Insects and mice held meetings in the laundry room, discussing claims on leftover crumbs and debris. Vacuum and broom all day occupies time and space 'til there's nothing left to do. Washing my face alone in the dark, I see emotional scars and modern-day fears of what's to come. Tearstains on my pillow cover the pain from so long ago. This prisoner inside is killing me silently. Will she ever go away?

American Tragedy #36: Political Turmoil

Three DFL candidates put everything on the line. Primary day is here. They rally the troops, and voters pick and choose. Two are bank-rolling their campaigns with personal wealth in the millions while the third rode in on the coattails of incumbents with full party endorsements.

Who would have thought two polar opposites would run so close on this historic night? Anxiety and celebration continued for hours for two of the DFL party camps as the third conceded early on. Midnight approached as percentage points whittled away confidence for the DFL party endorsee number three.

The lonely veteran stood patient and calm, waiting for all votes to be tallied. Respectful of his opponents, refused to give in to traditional victory temptations. Odds were stacked against the old wealthy recluse, sited for erratic behavior, reoccurring demons of depression, and alcohol addiction, they feared. Abandoned by DFL party leaders, he vowed to unite. "Tax the rich" slogan may become his legacy in this tight win-or-lose fight.

American Tragedy #37: Walk Away

The moment you touched my life was the moment I realized lives are too short to gamble away feelings we have for each other today. Let me know you still care. Are you willing to share? I may be a friend or a stranger in town, but I'll always love you and want you around.

Don't walk away from our love, woman; turn around before it's too late. Let's talk it over. We'll work it out. If we really love each other, there's nothing to worry about.

We're just two sensitive people so easily hurt, but a special kind of you and me together will make it work. I remember yesterday and how we dreamed of tomorrow—the joy of you and me together, the moments and the hours.

Don't walk away from our love, woman; turn around before it's too late. Let's talk it over. We'll work it out. If we really love each other, there's nothing to worry about.

American Tragedy #38: Legacies and Museums

Where do they come from, and where do they go once they have achieved it all? Perhaps they sail into the sunset to an island far away or remain hidden in a secluded forest surrounded by caregivers of hope?

Retail empires built with family fortunes and name recognition for giving so much to the community, but what to do when your working days are through? Acquire fine art and historical antiques, or perhaps secure instruments from all over the world?

Windfalls in the millions, they leap from their nests as perks and benefits flow on and on. To whom shall these earthly possessions in the billions go at life's end? So fragile and frail the earthly life we live, not even science can stop the internal aging process, it's said. The rich never forget tax-free waivers, nor do they shun political fundraisers. They love counting their money in bed.

He lived a life of luxury, keeping youthful in personal contacts and public relations. She waited patiently in the wings for her aging knight and his massive wealth. Fortunes may rise and fall in desperate economic times, but there will always be stories told of rich men who build legacies and museums of gold.

American Tragedy #39: So Long Ago

It seems so long ago; I felt so all alone and far away, but you came into my life and opened up my eyes, and together you and I will share our love.

You are a part of me when we are close together: someone who cares how I feel, to pick me up when life brings me down. And when the time is right, we hold each other and share our love.

When you smile and look my way, I feel so different inside. You're everything to me. I could never replace you. Just a promise from you that you'll never change—share our love, share our love, share our love—so long ago.

American Tragedy #40:
Where Should I Be?

I woke this morning from a dream I had. Something kept telling me I should be glad for all that I am and all that I see; another day passes by, still it's questioning me. Where should I be?

I know that I am an artist by trade, but for a song my living is made. Got my mind on the job with hesitation; my hands on my piano can see my destination. Where should I be?

Should I go it alone? Will I make it on my own? When I decide I've had enough of this ride, I'm going to settle down and write a song, let the world know I'm around.

If I had the time to get away from it all, out in the country on a lake I'd recall the places I've been to, the people I've seen, the changes I'm going through. What does it mean? Where should I be?

Should I go it alone? Will I make it on my own? When I decide I've had enough of this ride. I'm going to settle down and write a song, let the world know I'm around.

American Tragedy #41: Healthcare for All

Affordable healthcare: is there really such a thing? Too costly to fund and too controversial to support—that's all media reports. What about promoting diet and exercise and healthier lifestyles? Impossible, they say, for corporate merchants of soft drinks, candy, and fatty foods would go broke.

Follow the health trends of allies in Canada, Norway, and Sweden. They must be doing something right, for people are living longer and healthier lives. The secret is in living through modest means and less stress in forgoing pop culture marketing machines.

Of course, two choices remain for the skeptics in doubt: do nothing and leave coverage for the wealthy, pass out vouchers and coupons to health clubs, bicycles, and diet prescriptions to the poor.

American Tragedy #42: Closing In

I feel the world turning around me. Quiet nights, city lights are all I see. People hiding in their routine places, many disguises, still the same old faces.

Closing in, like a night that lasts forever, closing in like four walls that come together. Closing in, from the time I begin, I find my life is closing in.

Falling leaves on a breeze of winter's cry. Another autumn passes, I say goodbye. Where has the summer gone? Time keeps moving on.

Closing in, but the night can't last forever. Closing in, but four walls can't come together. Closing in, from the time I begin, I find my life is closing in.

It seems like love has abandoned me. Where, oh, where can it be? High above the clouded skies, I touch the starlight with my eyes.

Closing in, like a night that lasts forever, closing in, like four walls that come together. Closing in, from the time I begin, I find my life is closing in.

American Tragedy #43: Rewarding Corporate Malfeasance

Another scandal in the wind, news breaks: "Business as Usual in Corporate America." No big deal: it's just a CEO running with his shameless severance package entitlement. Thanks to his lawyers and over-anxious board, HP filled the briefcase of ousted Mark Herd with $28 million more.

Bow out gracefully, CEOs, before investigations, claims, and charges are filed. Spare shareholders and consumers your exiting embarrassment. Authority and trust you grossly defiled, still we reward you with millions for settling harassment charges mild.

Another scandal in the wind news breaks: "Business as Usual in Corporate America." No big deal: it's just a CEO running with his shameless severance package entitlement. Thanks to his lawyers and over-anxious board, BP filled the briefcase of ousted CEO Tony Hayward with $16.8 million more.

Another scandal in the wind news breaks: "Business as Usual in Corporate America." No big deal: it's just a CEO running with his shameless severance package entitlement. Thanks to the lawyers and over-anxious board, Merrill Lynch filled the briefcase of ousted CEO Stan O'Neal with $160 million more.

Another scandal in the wind news breaks: "Business as Usual in Corporate America." No big deal: it's just a CEO running with his shameless severance package entitlement. Thanks to the lawyers and over-anxious board, Home Depot filled the briefcase of ousted CEO Robert Nardelli with $210 million more.

Bow out gracefully, CEOs, before investigations, claims, and charges are filed. Spare shareholders and consumers your exiting embarrassment. Authority and trust you grossly defiled, still we reward you with millions for settling harassment charges mild.

American Tragedy #44: Goodbye, Friend

Times have not been good of late; friends have come and gone. Once they know your state of affairs, you're ridiculed and abandoned. Swallow your pride; there's nothing to envy, clothes are ragged and old. You show up at public libraries daily with empty pockets and visions of gold.

Met an old friend for coffee today. He picked up the tab, cutting his doughnut in half for two. Conversation was awkward at best; listening to his $500,000 high-yielding investment rollover was a bit nauseating. No debts and no children, a friend with nothing better to do. Brag about linguistic skills, private happy hours, and personal pleasures of taboo.

Weekly phone calls consist of friends leaving messages of dry humor and sarcasm. After one too many drinks consumed at home, he withdraws his friendship. Vulgar words exchanged, cursing rat falls back into his hole. What more can be said about a lonely man whose green card never expires?

American Tragedy #45: Love Thy Neighbor

Pounding on the front door, horn honking in the driveway, he's in a hurry once again. Could this be my worst nightmare or just a neighborhood friend? Small talk is short while criticisms run wild. He's always a pleasure to greet: a yard filled with old possessions and personal obsessions—there's nothing there to compete.

Borrowed my lawnmower the other day. Neighbor's mower was in a state of disrepair. Two hours went by, and there was a bang on the front door. Neighbor was smiling from ear to ear, for the joke was on me. Lawnmower tires full of dog droppings—what a neighborly thing to flee.

Neighbor stopped by for coffee the other day. Had some idle time on his hands. Rude comments and criticisms were made one after another—household furnishings and jobless circumstances. Neighbors living in glass houses should be careful of trash hidden behind backyard fences.

American Tragedy #46:
Face in the Crowd

Just another pretty face passes by me on a busy corner place. Some will smile, but others just don't have time enough to say hello. They all seem the same, standing in a crowd and small talking by name, comparing all the latest news, competing for the winning prize. No one really knows.

Growing up when people seemed to care. Understanding, the give and take was fair. A little old fashioned, I guess that's really me. Heart full of honesty brings love so close to me.

Just another pretty face. It's another town, a different place. Many want to know my name, and how they try to lead me on! They never seem to change. What a foolish game: life's a spinning wheel of misfortune and blame. You gamble on a beauty queen, giving all your love inside, for what—a deceptive scheme?

Growing up when people seemed to care. Understanding, the give and take was fair. A little old fashioned, I guess that's really me. Heart full of honesty brings love so close to me.

American Tragedy #47: Spare Change

Today was a special day for my father, my sister, and me. Going to the county fair was all I'd dreamed it would be. There were talent shows and pony rides, food vendors, and so much more. We saved all year long, and had plenty of coins in our pockets; my father even had spare change and few jobless curses, too.

It's been so long since we gathered just for fun, my father, my sister, and me, but these struggling times, I admit, are most difficult for remaining a family. Collecting coupons and visiting thrift stores have become a way of life. Pooling coins from our closets and garage sale toys can be such a pain, but nothing compares to backing out groceries in the checkout line as people watch you in shame.

American Tragedy #48: Flea Markets, Pawn Shops, Pizzas to Go

I know a man so carefree he comes and goes as he pleases. He has a real day job, clocking forty hours a week or so and a side job with fringe benefits of specialty sandwiches and pepper-jack cheese. No apologies for his exhaustion or temper flares running wild; at least he's gainfully employed.

Six days a week he works sunup 'til sundown, yet he still manages backyard chores, but on Sunday there's no rest for this weary—he's a man on the go. At the crack of dawn, he's shopping in flea markets and pawnshops, paying homage to pagan gods. Even street merchants know him by name.

At least he has two jobs to occupy his waking hours. Two paychecks and health coverage—what more could a man ask for? Perhaps a road trip to the prairie would do. For now, he'll keep working two or three menial jobs; take a nap in between so he doesn't hit the floor from exhaustion.

Friday nights are special: he volunteers at the local Legion. All-you-can-eat chicken dinners and free Budweiser beer go nicely on a budget. On alternating Friday nights, he buys an extra-large pizza to go. Love those take-and bake-pizzas that somehow end up in my oven. Nothing like pizza and off-brand barley pops, an obscure menu of choice. Talking gossip, spitting backyard profanity on my deck, to some, is quite neighborly.

American Tragedy #49: Record Low Rate

Not even record-low mortgage rates can break the silence in a failed economy. Where are the jobs? Send in the jobs! Don't bother; it's politics, they fear. Too much job uncertainty and surplus foreclosures have kept home-buyers at bay.

Realtors, quite desperate, are at a loss, not sure what to do. Lower interest rates or lower home prices—they leave it up to you to figure out. Misguided sellers drop their price two, three, and four times. Contract ends, house pulled off the market, realtor moves on. Discouraged and disappointed sellers wait for another day.

Unprecedented, they say: a historical debacle with low rates has done nothing to sway people to buy. High unemployment and lack of jobs does little to stir buyer confidence. Where are the jobs? Send in the jobs. Don't bother; it's politics, they fear.

American Tragedy #50:
Look at the Powerful People

Politicians rallied votes, some unwillingly forced to disrupt their summer breaks. Emergency call to order, for thousands of teachers', state, and local government workers' jobs were hanging in balance. Thanks to a little pressure from the union and Democratic Senate, a $26 billion jobs bill was passed.

It was never about the politics but saving American jobs, you see. Teachers and government workers always take priority over the lay people. After all, why would anyone want to be caught in a second recessional storm? Concern was not about politicians' re-election status. No, emphasis was placed on children's education.

Homeland Security received another major boost in support from the House as well. Senate passed a $600 million border security bill, too. Look at what powerful people can do when caring for a nation in need. They forever changed the lives of Katrina victims and Terri Schiavo, and resolved the Gulf oil disaster too.

American Tragedy #51: Forgive Me, Please

Could anything get any worse for the millions whose lives are on hold? Welfare checks, extended benefits, and fundraisers are fine, but what about a token of appreciation for those left behind?

Broken families, emotionally battered and bruised, find comfort in strange places. They curse each day and night, for everything gone wrong. What misery and shame! There never seems to be enough compassion or reconciliation—only bundles of regrets and plenty of blame to go around.

Was it him or her, them or they? So much bitterness and despair! Whatever happened to memorable days of weddings and birthdays so long ago? Promises made, covenants broken, everything left for chance. Love once shared has disappeared, and all that remains are dated Hallmark cards of yesterday's trivial romance.

American Tragedy #52:
All Felons Look Alike

White-collar criminals have become too American of late. It's hardly news of the day. Since 2002, many public leaders have fallen in disgrace. Some pardoned in office, and others given golden parachutes. Perks tendered openly for many, while very few hit bottom; to others sources of wealth rendered.

Dress these proud men up in government khakis or jumpsuits of orange or gold. Take a large group photo with wide-angle view—they all look like family to me. Uncle Bernie, Cousin Tom, have you seen Brother Denny today? Guards say he finished his chores in the mess hall and is playing cards in the man cave.

Warden says these fine, upstanding men never looked better in shiny brass belt buckles and polished black boots—my, how they glow! Bunk beds and dorm rooms are cleaned so well. Is scandal in the nation still on the rise? More investigations of theft, fraud, and corruption surface in business affairs, while a handful await their fate.

Another day behind bars: they feel no shame or remorse for all they have done. It was fun while it lasted. A good life they lived of making billions in fortune and fame. Still, some things bother a few when family and friends come to visit. Comments are often made: why do all felons look the same?

American Tragedy #53: Community Jobs Forum

Jobless and broke, I volunteered my time to host a Community Jobs Forum in the city. Several middle-age men and women braved sub-zero temperatures one cold winter night in January 2010. Still, all were hopeful their voices would be heard.

Two hours of lively debate and heated response were given in good faith by a non-political lay group of people who cared. Job-creation options were well documented and priority noted for White House records. Still, all were hopeful their voices would be heard.

As I wrapped up the meeting, thanking everyone for his/her contributions, couldn't help but feel their opinions really didn't matter. Main Street Americans have nothing in common with government agendas. Still, all were hopeful their voices would be heard.

No state or federal politicians knew or cared we even participated that dark, cold winter night. Months passed, and nothing transpired—not even a simple reply. We lacked endorsements, private funding, and mass media support. Still, all were hopeful their voices would be heard.

American Tragedy #54: Sail Away on Broken Dreams

Small businesses come and go, as do the ebb and flow of prosperous stock markets. Loss, for some, means a slight reduction in surplus wealth; for others, total devastation. Still, at the end of the day, all that's left are shattered pieces of a man's broken dreams.

Jobless, homeless, helpless people, when will you earn your way out of poverty? Surely, you must know you've become too dependent on food shelves, shelters, and public assistance. Still, at the end of the day, all that's left are shattered pieces of a man's broken dreams.

Human Rights Day, Bill of Rights Day, Human Rights Week: what does this mean to Americans denied ideals? America hasn't always sided with the innocent or oppressed, begging for equality. Still, at the end of the day, all that's left are shattered pieces of a man's broken dreams.

American Tragedy #55: Peace Behind the Curtain

After months of heavy rain, thunder, and lightning, storm clouds finally disappeared. Sunlit rooms brought rays of hope and promises of better days ahead. Friends told me to let bygones be bygones, let sleeping dogs lie for today.

They said I'd find no peace in this broken home, only sleepless nights and torment. At times, it felt not even prayer could ease the pain of loneliness and depression. Was it the bitter poison of a wicked snake bite from so long ago?

Day lilies and mourning doves fill my backyard with hope. Even sacred crows stop and smell the roses where river birch once grew. No one knows the life one lives behind the curtained wall. Thanks to God, for I found peace in the silent wind.

American Tragedy #56: No One to Depend On

August was the hottest month on record. So glad it cooled down today. Even the dog howled, thankful for the cool breeze. Nothing can beat the heat like cross winds blowing through red oak trees. It's just me alone and no one else, you see.

Up at 3:00 o'clock this morning, I thought I heard my daughter calling. Turned the hall light on and let the dog out; saw a bobcat chase a stray owl away. Dark night, pale moonlight; has anyone seen my dog? It's just me alone and no one else, you see.

Everything's calm this evening, watching time fly. Mosquitoes chatting with moths as mice chase street cats outside my window. Gossiping neighbors stop and stare down the driveway, looking for signs of new life. It's just me alone and no one else, you see.

Photographs of children hang on the walls; they remind me of family I once knew. Thanksgiving feasts and Christmas Eve gatherings are joyful memories gone by. Empty rooms of dust-filled furniture are all that remains. It's just me alone and no one else, you see.

American Tragedy #57:
Flickering Lights,
Smoldering Ashes

Candlelit sunroom, movie playing on the wide screen, a little popcorn for two. Uncork some Merlot and a slice of Gouda. Feeling stressed today. They snuggled so close, sharing romantic thoughts for the moment. Excuse the dog's interruption; she's only begging for more loose kernels of corn.

Out on the patio, they went to see candlelit torches all aglow. Fire pit burns brightly on a moonlit night, perfect for star-gazing. Warm summer breeze stirring oak leaves; fireflies put on a show for two. Pour another glass of Merlot—we'll swing by the lake, watching the moon glow.

It's two in the morning; all the candles have died out except one flickering in the window. Hugging and kissing, they walk down the stairs embracing each other as he says goodbye. Front door opens and closes, outside lights blink three times as they thank each other for the wonderful dinner date.

Smoke rises from the backyard fire pit, ashes smoldering in the wind. Scattered bottles and corks under glass signal another romantic affair. Lonely hearts share secrets of broken promises made so long ago. Too much Merlot medicates the mind's cloud-filled thoughts and idealized wishes of dreams that will never come true.

American Tragedy #58:
Finally Got Rid of Him

After years of misery, the drama and chaos finally ended. She went her way, cursing and kicking all the way out the front door. Her last words: "won't this guy ever leave my house?" Nothing lasts forever, no bargains in life, at least not with him.

Bittersweet memories: children recall days living with her and him. Hidden boxes of photographs scattered everywhere—family, relatives, and pictures of her and him, too. Yard signs lined the streets with foreclosures and forced home sales.

She finally struck gold, falling into the arms of plenty while he quietly embraced solitude and poverty. Ultimately, her means did justify an unhappy ending. Although not a pretty sight, she finally got rid of him.

American Tragedy #59:
Wine, Romance, and Dinner, Too

Stopped by the house the other night. Sweet smell of spices, olive oil, and baked salmon filled the air. Doorbell rang and a knock on the front door—company's here. The dog barks as she welcomes her guest—all the way from downtown, too.

Corks popping, wine pouring, Merlot toasting for two. What's this odd celebration that makes life so sweet? Love hasn't lived here for quite some time. Where are the children tonight? Have they gone with the in-laws, too?

"Pass the French bread. I'll turn on some romantic music," she said with a smile.

"Maybe we could slow dance for a song or two," he replied. Love the flowers and attention you bring me. She knows the way into his heart tonight—good wine, romance, and dinner, too.

American Tragedy #60: Silent Nights

More vacant homes have popped up in the neighborhood since the recession began. Jobless neighbors we knew divorced and disappeared, never to be seen again. Some died or moved away, while others just left out of shame and embarrassment.

Days have grown shorter, nights longer, as fall settles in with a chill. Raccoons and squirrels scour the streets, looking for leftovers. There used to be block parties and family gatherings—not so much anymore. Silence has killed the spirit in the wind.

Where have the white squirrels gone, once living in red oak trees? Robins abandon their nests for reasons not even science knows. This old house is so dark and cold looking now. Even the outside lights are burnt out, except for the one on the right.

American Tragedy #61: Whispering, Kissing Down the Hallway

Tired, he went to bed early the other night—was feeling the stress of it all. The day was long, and jobs were far and few to qualify. Workforce centers and social job sites leave much to be desired as response to applications post zero. No one knows he's here tonight, asleep in the room below.

Dreaming, his mind took him elsewhere tonight. Car lights shined brightly outside the upper window. Voices laughing, a key opened the door. "Who could that be at this hour?" No one knows he's here tonight, asleep in the room below.

The car pulled away, or so he thought for a moment. Still, he heard sounds of strange, whispering voices. Everything was quiet, and suddenly he heard whispering words of passion and kissing down the hallway. No one knows he's here tonight, asleep in the room below.

Sounds of footsteps coming down the stairs, a chauffeured limousine idles outside. Whisperings of "I love you" and kisses from the fisher king to his queen. The door opens quickly and closes while the lights flicker on/off three times. Suddenly they vanish from sight. No one knows he was here tonight, asleep in the room below.

American Tragedy #62: Vigilante Granny

Passed by a vacant house the other day—was on a dog walk for therapy. Some say a family full of spirit and life once lived there, or so I hear. Now all that remains are lingering stories of an angry old recluse—so bitter and reviled was she.

On a clear summer's day, one could hear voices of laughter on one side of the house and shouts of vulgar obscenities on the other. Was it the stress from him or her, the economy, the recession, or investments gone wrong? What caused this granny to become so vigilante?

Neighbors recall birthdays, graduations, and welcome parties from days gone by. Grandchildren came with gifts and good news, colorful balloons everywhere. As the years passed by, hardly ever a kind word rolled off her lips. She blames the misery on him.

Perhaps what gnawed away inside her narrow mind was unresolved pride and revenge. Curse the day she met him for making false promises of dreams that never came true. She vowed one day to get even for all the misery she endured.

American Tragedy #63: Missing Family Reunions

Since Mother and Dad passed away years ago, family reunions are not the same anymore. Some of us try to gather every once in a while, but relatives keep passing away, too.

Miss the sweet aroma of rigatoni, simmering hot Italian sausage, and grated Romano cheese—such rich family tradition. Stories and jokes of growing up on Spaghetti Hill still make me smile.

So much has happened over the years; broken promises, delayed obligations cause alienation within. Failed economy and personal tragedies have all contributed to the sufferings and pain felt by many families in transition.

Not everyone can understand the burden one carries. Still, a few reach out in compassionate ways. Often, guilt and shame overcome daily thoughts, preventing some from gathering. Others try embarrassing excuses to avoid being caught in a lie.

American Tragedy #64: Terminally Still

Telephones are ringing in my head. Who's calling me today? Bill collectors or jobless friends seeking recipes for potato soup? Anxiety attacks reoccurring of late—it's raining again, too. Hope this dreary day hasn't sealed my fate.

People gather outside my front door. What is this strange parade? Don't recognize anyone except two sisters weeping beyond. Where are all the lights in this cold house? Won't someone at least turn one on?

Cars lined up single-file, moving slowly with headlights on. A neighbor waves goodbye as he wipes the tears away. Autumn fields are empty this morning; the wheat has all been harvested. Until we meet again, my friends, may peace be with you all.

American Tragedy #65: Rainbows in My Backyard

Today was a special day. We celebrated our sunroom addition. We planted apple trees and built a swing set of rainbow colors and more. Planned our first garden party with a trampoline filled with balloons and cotton candy dreams for my children.

So much we are blessed to live in a house of promises and hope. Storms may come and go, but rainbows always appear in my backyard. Twenty-four years have passed, and still colors of red, yellow, and blue filter through the rain.

My mind still wanders back to that place I once called a happy home. That's where my family dreams were made. No bad economy or personal tragedy can ever take away the fond memories of climbing rainbows in my back yard.

Conclusion

Could this Great Recession and all these personal tragedies been prevented? It's debatable for some, while most would say, emphatically, "Yes." Lack of character, excessive greed, ego, and failed leadership caused this American tragedy. Millions suffered the consequences for the actions of a few. Rewards for failure still flow from the boardrooms on down to fallen CEOs, while the lives of many are destroyed.

Does anyone in government or corporate America really know what it's like to live jobless and homeless in a nation so rich? If you could afford to live without pay for a month and still maintain a luxurious lifestyle, you haven't a clue what it means to live in poverty. While it's admirable when the world's richest billionaires propose giving half their wealth to charity, they will never suffer the loss or go hungry, homeless, jobless, or hopeless in America, as millions have and continue to do.

The rich have everything they want except happiness, and the poor are sacrificed to the unhappiness of the rich.
Thomas Merton

Perhaps we all could gain a better understanding of those truly in need of our help and human compassion. Mother Teresa's selfless giving of herself and caring for the poor were examples of genuine humility in action.

Mother Teresa's Poem

People are often unreasonable, illogical and self-centered; forgive them anyway.

If you are kind, people may accuse you of selfish, ulterior motives; be kind anyway.

If you are successful, you will win some false friends and some true enemies; succeed anyway. If you are honest and frank, people may cheat you; be honest and frank anyway. What you spend years building, someone could destroy overnight; build anyway. If you find serenity and happiness, they may be jealous; be happy anyway. The good you do today, people will forget tomorrow, do good anyway. Give the world the best you have, and it may never be enough; give the world the best you've got anyway. You see, in the final analysis, it is between you and God; it never was between you and them anyway.

I cannot change what has happened to my family or me in recent years, but I can change how I react to disparity and lack of opportunity for those in need. Words of encouragement and doors opening—employment opportunities—are what jobless people need in this country. America cannot afford another recession or financial disaster like the one it's in currently. It's time to support the basic needs and rights of all U.S. citizens by helping them find jobs that pay living wages. Affordable housing and healthcare of some kind must become available to families struggling to live the American dream. This is not too much to ask for in a nation filled with abundant wealth and natural resources. All it takes is a small group of individuals willing to band together to create economic opportunities in every city and town across America. We bailed out Wall Street in the billions, mounted trillions in deficit debt, and survived 9/11, and all the corporate fraud, greed, and corruption from Enron to Bernie Madoff. Possibilities exist for bringing honest Americans back to work and back to owning homes in this country where hopes and dreams were once made. This is more than realistic—it's doable today.

"There are better things ahead than any we left behind."
C.S. Lewis

References

Quotes To Ponder

Obama signs massive tax bill, hails deal with GOP. (2010, December 17). MSNBC.Com. Retrieved December 18, 2010 from http://www.msnbc.com/id/40697296/ns/politics-capitol_hill/

Olson, J. (2010, September 28). Census reveals 'new poor' in many Twin Cities suburbs. StarTribune.com. Retrieved September 30, 2010, from http://www.startribune.com/templates/fdcp?1285893659123

Pelley, S. (2010, December 5). Fed Chairman Ben Bernanke's Take On The Economy. CBS News, *Minutes.* Retrieved December 6, 2010, from http://www.cbsnews.com/stories/2010/12/03/60minutes/main7114229

Stassen-Berger, R. (2011, January 6). Dayton stands his ground on taxes with business groups. StarTribune.Com. Retrieved January 7, 2011, from http://www.startribune.com/templates/fdcp?1294418984476

Superville, D. (2010, September 4). US needs 'thriving middle class,' Obama says; GOP renews attack on gov't rules, regulations. Retrieved September 4, 2010, from http://www.startribune.com/templates/fdcp?1283615410813

Dedication

The New American Bible. (1970, July 27). 1 Corinthians 2: 14-16 (NAB), p. 1262. New York: Thomas Nelson.

Introduction

Blanchard, K., Carlos, J.P., Randolph, A. (1996). *Empowerment takes more than a minute.* (p. 49). San Francisco, CA: Berrett-Koehler.

House set to approve jobless benefits extension. *Associated Press. Retrieved* July 22, 2010, from http://www.msnbc.com/id/38362070/ns/business-stocks_economy/

Tragedy #2

Hansen, C. (2009, February 8). Where's the money? A look at bailout. *Dateline NBC* Retrieved February 9, 2009, from http://www.msnbc.com/id/29088710/print/1/displaymode/1098/

Pelley, S. (2008, September 28). Paulson Warns Of Fragile Economy. *CBS News, 60 Minutes.* Retrieved September 29, 2008, from http://www.cbsnews.com/Stories/2008/09/28/60minutes/printable4483612.shtml

Tragedy #3

Major CEOs feeling the recession . . . somewhat. *Associated Press.* Retrieved May 1, 2009, from http://www.msnbc.msn.com/id/30501718/print/1/displaymode/1098/

Tragedy #5

Arbel, T. Economy sheds 345,000 jobs . . . *Associated Press.* Retrieved June 6, 2009, from http://www.startribune.com/business/47039162.html?page=2&c=y

Economy sheds more jobs than expected. *Associated Press and Reuters*. Retrieved January 8, 2010, from http://www.msnbc.msn.com/id/34764269/ns/business-stocks_and_economy/print/1/displaymode/1098/

Rugaber, C.S. Despite some hiring . . . Associated Press. Retrieved September 4, 2010, from http://www.startribune.com/business/102142764.html

Temp work covers up depth of unemployment. Associated Press. Retrieved June 9, 2010, from http://www.msnbc.msn.com/id/31127909/print/1/displaymode/1098/

Tragedy #6

Watchdog wants banks to report TARP usage. Associated Press. Retrieved July 19, 2009, from http://www.msnbc.msn.com/id/31994686/ns/business-us_business/print/1/displaymode/1098/

Wagner, D. (2009, October 15). Watchdog puts Geithner in hot seat over AIG. *Star Tribune*, Business, D3.

Walsh, MW et al. (2009, March 16). A.I.G. Lists Banks It Paid With U.S. Bailout Funds. *The New York Times*. Retrieved March 17, 2009, from http://www.nytimes.com/2009/03/16/business/16rescue.html?_r=1&page wanted=print

Tragedy #9

Kroft, S. (2009, March 1). The Man Who Figured Out Madoff's Scheme. *CBS News, 60 Minutes*. Retrieved March 2, 2009, from http://www.cbsnews.com/stories/2009/02/27/60minutes/main/4833667.shtml.

SEC watchdog: Madoff 'got away lucky' in 06. *Associated Press*. Retrieved September 5, 2009, from http://www.msnbc.msn.com/id/32701060/ns/business-us_business/print/1/displaymode/1098/

Tragedy #12

Fedor, L., Phelps, D. (2009, December 3). Petters guilty: Trail tapes, betrayal led to verdict. *Star Tribune.* Retrieved December 3, 2009, from http://www.startribune.com/local/78263722.html?page=5&c=y

Kroft, S. (2009, October 25). Medicare Fraud: A $60 Billion Crime. *CBS News, 60 Minutes.* Retrieved October 26, 2009, from http://www.cbsnews.com.stories/2009/10/23/60minutes/main5414390.shtml? Tag=contentMain;cbsCarou . . .

Once high-flying NYC lawyer sentenced to 20 years in $400 million fraud. *Star Tribune.* Retrieved July 15, 2009, from http://www.startribune.com/business/50673092.html?page=2&c=y

Tragedy #15

Federal Trade Commission. (2008). File No. 0623063, *News Release* December 16, 2008. Mortgage Lender Agrees to Settle FTC Charges That It Charged African-Americans and Hispanics Higher Prices for Loans. Retrieved August 17, 2010, from http://www.ftc.gov/opa/2008/12/gateway.shtm

Williams, B. (2009, April 10). Minneapolis settles bias lawsuit by black officers *Minnesota Public Radio News*. Retrieved

August 17, 2010, from http://minnesota.publicradio.org/display/web/2009/04/10/copslawsuit_ settlement/.

Yee, C.M. (2008, September 11). Former United Health Care CEO Settles Lawsuit. *Star Tribune*. Retrieved August 17, 2010, from http://www.startribune.com/28136419.html/?page=1&c=y

Tragedy #17

American Recovery and Reinvestment Act of 2009. *Conference Report of the United States Congress.* Retrieved August 2, 2010, from http://www.themiddleclass.org/bill/american-recovery-and-reinvestment-act-2009-conference-report?gclid . . .

Tragedy #18

O'Grady, K. (2010, July 23). President Signs Unemployment Extension into Law. Charleston Unemployment Benefits Examiner. Retrieved August 2, 2010, from http://www.examiner.com/x-52174-Charleston-Unemployment-Benefits-Examiner~y2010m7d23-Presiden . . .

Tragedy #23

Aversa, J. (2009, July 17). Jobless rate tops 10 percent in 15 states and DC, endangers economic recovery. *Associated Press.* Retrieved July 18, 2009, from http://www.startribune.com/business/51026592.html?elr=KArksUUUoDEy3LGDio7aiU.

Unemployment rate soars to 8.1 percent. *Associated Press.* Retrieved March 6, 2009, from http://www.msnbc.msn.com/id/29538287/print/1/displaymode/1098/.

Unemployment rate rises above 10 percent. *Associated Press.* Retrieved November 6, 2009, from http://www.msnbc. msn.com/id/33713864/ns/business-personal_finance/ print/1/displaymode/1098/.

Weekly jobless claims up more than expected. *Associated Press.* Retrieved April 23, 2009, from http://www.msnbc. msn.com/id/30364714/print/1/displaymode/

Tragedy #25

Number of Vacant Homes in U.S. Hits 19 Million. *Huffington Post.* Retrieved August 4, 2010, from http://www. huffingtonpost.com/2010/04/26/number-of-vacant- homes-in_n_552274.html?view=print.

Mutikani, L. (2009, September 10). U.S. poverty rate hits 11-year high. *Reuters.* Retrieved August 4, 2010, from http://www. reuters.com/assesys/print?aid=USTRE58943C20090910.

Record number of Americans living in poverty. *Associated Press, MSNBC.* Retrieved September 17, 2010, from http:// www.msnbc.msn.com/id/39211644/ns/us_news-life/

Tragedy #26

Citigroup. Goldman Sachs Group Inc. (2009, October 16). *Star Tribune,* Nation + World, Business D3.

Kennedy, P. (2010, March 5). CEO PAY WATCH ECOLAB INC. *Star Tribune,* business, D1.

Tragedy #28

Cornelius, D. (2009, December 17). Credit Sussie Settles OFAC Charges for $536 million, *Compliance Building.* Retrieved

August 17, 2010, from http://www.compliancebuilding. com/2009/12/17/credit-sussie-settles-ofac-charges-for-536- million/

Goldman, D. (2010, August 4). Intel Settles antitrust suit with wrist slap. *CNN Money*. Retrieved August 17, 2010, from http://money.cnn.com/2010/08/04/-technology/intel_ftc_ settlement/index.htm

Tragedy #30

U.S. Equal Employment Opportunity Commission Report. (2010). *Job Bias Charges Approach Record High in Fiscal Year 2009, EEOC Reports*. Retrieved March 20, 2010, from http:// www.eeoc.gov/eeoc/newsroom/release/1-6-10.cfm

Tragedy 31

Gross, D. (2010, April 9). The Comeback Country. Newsweek. Retrieved August 7, 2010, from http://www.newsweek. com/2010/04/08/the-comeback-country.print.html

Tragedy #34

Foster, M., Skoloff, B. (2010, August 7). Gulf seafood industry tries to shake an oily Image. *Associated Press*. Retrieved August 7, 2010, from http://www.msnbc.msn.com/ cleanprint/CleanPrintProxy.aspx?12811202977306

Tragedy #43

Tahmincioglu, E. (2010, August 10). Business as usual: Princely payout for HP chief. *msnbc.com*. Retrieved August 10, 2010, from http://www.msnbc.msn.com/id/38631683/ns/ business-us_business/

Tragedy #50

Abrams, J. (2010, August 9). House members return to vote on jobs bill for teachers and government workers. *Associated Press*. Retrieved August 10, 2010, from http://www.startribune.com/templates/fdcp?1281454611364

Tragedy #54

The White House. (2009). *Presidential Proclamation—Human Rights Day, Bill of Rights Day, and Human Rights Week.* Retrieved January 6, 2010, from http://www.whitehouse.gov/the-press-office/presidential-proclamation-human-rights-day-bill-rights-day-an . . .

Conclusion

Lewis, C.S. (1968). Quotations: *There are better things ahead . . .).* Retrieved September 3, 2010, from http://www.anglik.net/lewis.htm.

Merton, T. (2008). Choosing to love the world on contemplation. Boulder, CO: Sounds True.

Teresa, M. (1997). Mother Teresa's Poem: Do It Anyway. Retrieved August 11, 2010, from http://www.maryourmother.net/Teresa.html/

Back Cover

Merton, T. (2008). Choosing to love the world on contemplation. Boulder, CO: Sounds True.

Msnbc.com. Obama signs massive tax bill . . . Retrieved December 18, 2010, from http://www.msnbc.msn.com/id/40697296/ns/politics-capitol_hill/

Pelley, S. (2010, December 5). Fed Chairman Ben Bernanke's Take On The Economy. CBS News, *60 Minutes*. Retrieved December 6, 2010, from http://www.cbsnews.com/stories/2010/12/03/60minutes/main7114229 . . .

Wayman, R. (2010, September 20). StarTribune.com. Letter of the day: Which candidate for governor will best fight rising poverty? Retrieved November 9, 2010, from http://www.startribune.com/templates/fdcp?1289335331907